When Prayers Are Answered

Amy Newmark

CSS

Chicken Soup for the Soul, LLC
Cos Cob, CT

Chicken Soup for the Soul: When Prayers Are Answered
Amy Newmark
Published by Chicken Soup for the Soul, LLC www.chickensoup.com

Copyright ©2017 by Chicken Soup for the Soul, LLC. All Rights Reserved.

The publisher gratefully acknowledges the many publishers and individuals who granted Chicken Soup for the Soul permission to reprint the cited material.

Front cover and back cover photo courtesy of iStockPhoto.com/Atropat (©Atropat).
Interior photo of Amy Newmark courtesy of Susan Morrow at SwickPix

Cover and Interior by Daniel Zaccari

ISBN: 978-1-61159-064-7

PRINTED IN THE UNITED STATES OF AMERICA
on acid∞free paper

25 24 23 22 21 20 19   03 04 05 06 07 08 09 10 11

Table of Contents

Expect Miracles

Miracles happen to those who believe in them.
~Bernard Berenson

During the Rwandan genocide of 1994 more than a million people were murdered in three months; by the grace of God, I was not one of them. At the time I was a twenty-four-year-old university student visiting home on Easter vacation when the long-brewing tribal hatred in my African homeland erupted into an unspeakable slaughter of innocents. When the killers arrived at our doorstep, my dad sent me running to a neighboring pastor for protection.

For the next ninety-one days I cowered in a

hidden, tiny bathroom with seven other terrified women while rapists and murderers relentlessly hunted for us. I opened my heart to God and prayed night and day that He spare my life and also, spare my soul, and not allow the hatred I felt for the killers to turn my heart to stone.

God heard my prayers and answered them.

Whenever the death squads ransacked the pastor's house searching for us, God blinded them from seeing the bathroom door and finding us.

Three months later, the genocide was over and I came out of hiding. I was emaciated, but alive. My heart was sad and I wanted the killers brought to justice, but I wasn't filled with poisonous hatred. On the contrary, to my amazement, I was ready to love and forgive.

With those prayers answered, I thought I'd used up a lifetime allotment of miracles. But I was wrong.

Outside the bathroom, the world I had known was gone. My once breathtakingly beautiful homeland had been transformed into a grotesque landscape of death and destruction. All my neighbors and my immediate family, with the exception of one brother who was living abroad, had been viciously murdered. My childhood home, which my father had built with his own hands as a wedding gift to my mother, had been burned to the ground. All I saw was the smoldering ruins of burnt out houses and a countryside strewn with corpses.

I had gone from being a happily pampered, only daughter to a starving orphaned refugee.

With no money, food or a single friend left alive, I made my way toward the Rwandan capital of Kigali in hopes of finding work, but there was none. No stores or businesses were open, there was virtually no power, no buses were running, there was precious little clean water to drink, the roads were littered with leftover landmines and wild dogs fed on the bodies that still lay in the street.

On my way to the city, I met and joined a band of fellow refugees at a temporary camp for displaced persons. One woman in the group owned a house in

Kigali, so at least I had a roof over my head—but we had no food and faced starvation. The only remote possibility of employment was secretarial work at the United Nations office that had just reopened. Unfortunately, I didn't speak English, I couldn't type, the only clothes I owned were the rags on my back and I hadn't had a bath in months. On top of that, the United Nations wasn't hiring, and even if it was, it had a long-standing policy of not hiring Rwandans.

Nevertheless, I walked the dangerous footpath to the UN every day to fill out a job application. Every day, they told me not to come back because they had no jobs. But I continued this routine for weeks until my legs buckled beneath me one day, not strong enough to keep walking to a job that didn't exist. I sank to my knees on the charred brick and broken glass of the ruined city in despair, and once again opened my heart to God.

"Lord, you have given me so much already, and I wouldn't ask for your help unless I truly needed it, but I need it Lord! I don't know what else to do. I have no money, my clothes are falling apart, and no one will give me a job. I know you didn't save me from the killers to let me starve to death in the streets. Help me find a way to make these UN people notice me and give me a job! I don't think I can last much longer."

I stood up and brushed myself off, certain God would answer my prayer — and I wanted to be ready when He did. I trusted He would arrange for me to have an interview at the UN, so I would need my high school diploma and some presentable clothes. The only place I could possibly find both would be my university dorm room more than 200 miles away and completely impossible for me get to.

At that very moment a car pulled up beside me and the driver rolled down his window.

"Immaculée, is that you? I hardly recognized you, you are so skinny now. I'm so happy you survived. Can I drive you anywhere?"

I couldn't believe my eyes and ears. It was one

of my professors from the university and he just happened to be making the five-hour drive to the campus!

I arrived at the university the next day and the dorm was in shambles; the door of my room had been heaved in with an axe and all my clothes and books had been stolen.

Everything was gone, except for a single envelope on the floor. It must have fallen beneath the bed when the looters pillaged the room. I picked it up and opened it… to find all my school records and $30 from my scholarship award! Suddenly, I was rich! I had enough cash to hire a taxi back to Kigali, with money left over.

When I returned to the city, two shops had reopened near my house while I was gone — a secondhand clothing store where I purchased a new outfit, and a beauty salon where I had my hair done. On the way home I used the last few dollars to buy groceries to feed all my housemates for a week.

A few days later my prayer was answered in

full — after an interview, I was picked to start a new job at the United Nations.

I also started a new life, knowing that whenever I opened my heart to God I could expect miracles.

~Immaculée Ilibagiza with Steve Erwin

Before the Baby Comes

*A baby is God's opinion that
the world should go on.*
~Carl Sandburg

onna was the first friend I made after moving from Vermont to Nashville in 1986. Since we both worked in the medical field and enjoyed walking, gardening, and laughing, she quickly became a dear friend. Besides attending a weekly church group together, we hoofed it around the Vanderbilt track on a regular basis in our usual fruitless effort to lose weight.

Donna had always wanted to be a mother but for five frustrating years nothing had happened despite Pergonal shots and endometriosis surgery. We all rejoiced when she finally conceived, but then at three months, the unthinkable happened — she miscarried. I cried with her at the painful loss of her baby and her hope. The painful saga continued into year six: every month starting hopeful but ending with bitter disappointment. Since I knew she and her husband would make ideal parents, I prayed (along with her family and church group), but no further pregnancies occurred.

Unlike Donna, I was ambivalent about motherhood. Did I really want to lose all my free time, money, and sleep? Did I want to deal with nasty diapers and whining? What if I turned into a cranky, inept mother? What if my children turned into selfish brats, drug addicts, or pedophiles? I was afraid to rock the boat, or in this case, the cradle!

My husband, however, wanted children and I knew he'd make a fantastic father. When I turned thirty-one, my husband tossed out the gentle hint: "You're not getting any younger, dear." As a doctor, I already knew birth defect rates increased after age thirty-five, and with Donna's experience, that conceiving could take years. I decided to just let nature take its course. "We're not going to try," I insisted. "We're just not going to prevent it — if it's meant to happen, it will." I figured with our hectic schedules, it would takes months, maybe even years.

Wrong! Try one month! I couldn't believe it when the very first month I got off birth control I conceived. My husband bounced around the room while I retched into the toilet, nauseated and in shock.

Once I was over the morning sickness, I warmed up to the idea of motherhood, except for the overwhelming guilt that consumed me every time I walked the track with Donna. Why me and not her? She had yearned for a baby for years and had tried so hard. I got pregnant the first month. It wasn't fair. It wasn't right, and I dreaded telling her.

In fact, for months I didn't! Instead, I begged God to bless her with a pregnancy before I had to tell her. But by my sixth month, I was showing and couldn't delay anymore. When I told her, she cried. "I didn't even know you wanted a baby." Talk about guilt.

I petitioned God even more on her behalf. I researched promising scripture verses and all the Old Testament stories of infertile women who eventually conceived: Sarah, Rebekah, Rachel, and Leah. As I prayed, I begged God to bless Donna, just as He had blessed these Old Testament matriarchs. I also added a caveat: Please make it happen before my baby is born. I knew it would be difficult for her to watch me with my newborn, and the last thing I wanted to do was hurt her or put a wedge in our friendship. Day and night I uttered the same prayer: "Bless Donna with a baby, and let her conceive before my baby is born." It became my mantra.

Eight months into my pregnancy, my water broke and nine hours later, at 8 a.m. on October

4th, my wonderful son, Steven, made his debut. Instant love and joy flowed through me as I gazed at my adorable little boy, a true blessing from God.

Once Steven was asleep, Nate and I called our friends and family with the news. I dreaded calling Donna. In fact, she was the last phone call I made because I was disappointed with God. Never had I prayed with as much faith, consistency, or fervor as I had prayed for Donna. But I had nothing to show for it. It had all been a waste of time. I made the dreaded call, and she promised to come by later that day.

After oohing and ahhing and agreeing that yes, Steven was the cutest baby on the face of the earth, Donna said, "There's something I'm dying to tell you. I found out at 7:00 this morning that I'm pregnant!"

My mouth dropped. She was pregnant? Tears welled in my eyes and I couldn't stop grinning. God not only answered my prayer, but timed it to the very hour!

Of course, I knew I wasn't the only one praying

for Donna. Her husband, family, friends, prayer group, and even a missionary in Japan were all lifting up prayers and petitions daily. Some had fasted. But that God had timed it to the very hour before my son was born was God's special blessing.

Nine months later, Donna delivered a healthy, beautiful baby girl who she named Michelle. Michelle is now a beautiful twenty-two-year-old missionary and will marry this spring.

~Sally Willard Burbank

Faith Happens

*Faith is not without worry or care, but
faith is fear that has said a prayer.*
~Author Unknown

There was no mistaking the lopsided thump my husband, seven-year-old son and I felt as we traveled home from the mall one Saturday afternoon; we had a flat tire. This was the first long outing we had taken since recently acquiring the car from my father. My husband had wanted to stay home that day and watch sports, but I had convinced him that family time at the mall would be more entertaining.

After turning on the hazard lights, my husband

guided our car safely to the side of the road. Since we were on the interstate, other vehicles seemed to zoom past us at record speeds, and I worried for my husband's safety since he would be changing the tire so near those speeding vehicles. "What are you looking for?" I finally asked after watching him rifle frantically through the glove box.

"There is a special tool made for this particular car that I have to use for tire changing. I put it in the glove box in case we ever needed to use it," he answered, still deeply engrossed in his search.

Should I tell him I had already seen the "special tool," and had removed it thinking it was something my father had accidentally left behind? Wouldn't it be better to allow him to believe that he had forgotten to place the tool in the glove box? After all, I was the one who had insisted we take this jaunt to the mall in the first place; he had wanted to stay home and watch the game. Finally I mustered enough courage to confess my crime. "Was it a little metal thingy shaped like an L?" I asked, innocently.

"Yeah, that's it. Have you seen it?" he asked. Several alternate explanations raced through my mind as possible means of salvation. I was leaning toward the "mugger snatching it from me as I sat cleaning it in the grocery store parking lot" scenario when I finally blurted, "Oh... I thought Daddy had accidentally left that in the car, and I put it on top of the fridge so we could give it back to him."

There it was. I had confessed my crime and waited for the consequences. I received a look of disgust and disbelief followed by the silent treatment.

With no tool to change the tire, we had only two options: call a wrecker and spend money we didn't really have, or continue at a snail's pace, with the hazard lights flashing, and chance ruining the wheel.

After what seemed to be hours (but was more like several minutes) of slowly thumping down the interstate, my seven-year-old, who had been unusually quiet this entire time, offered some advice. "Mom, Dad... we could pray," he suggested.

The look of frustration and impatience on my husband's face seemed to mirror my own feelings, and I noticed his jaw muscle jump ever so slightly beneath his skin. Of course we could pray, but this wasn't the type of situation to pray about… not when there were far more dire situations in the world that needed God's attention. Besides, how could prayer solve our problem? Would our tire miraculously heal itself and become plump with new air? "Okay, son," I said. I sounded tired. "You sit back and pray."

With each metallic crunch and thud, I felt myself tense against the sound and shift toward the "good side" of the car. Somehow it seemed there would be less weight on the tire if I held my breath. I didn't really believe that, of course, but I found myself involuntarily wincing after each fatal clunk anyway.

A few motorists actually slowed down and offered their help, but none of them had the "special tool" necessary for changing tires on our particular car. It finally got to the point where we wished people would just stop asking. Our luck changed, however, when a large white pickup truck passed us and then stopped on the side of the road. It looked promising, so we eased our car over next to the truck as its doors swung open and five men — all wearing the same sort of T-shirt — bounded out. Our disgruntled attitudes were in stark contrast to their ear-to-ear smiles, and they all seemed overly anxious to help us. The part I found most peculiar was they just so happened to have the specific tool necessary to change a tire on our car. And boy, were they fast! They had the flat tire off and the spare on in a matter of seconds, it seemed. Their smiles never left their faces, even as they loaded our flat tire into our trunk, and told us to have a nice day.

Everything happened so quickly and in such a surreal way that my husband and I just sat dumbfounded watching the men, one by one, pile back into their truck and wave goodbye. Then we heard a small voice from the back seat: "I told you we should pray." I glanced up just in time to see the truck's bumper sticker before it disappeared in the distance. It read, "Faith Happens."

~Cynthia Zayn

Circle of Prayer

*Prayer is not eloquence, but earnestness; not
the definition of helplessness, but the
feeling of it; not figures of speech,
but earnestness of soul.*
~Hannah More

Most likely, the doctor found the first birthday card startling. I pictured him pausing, trying to pinpoint my motivation, before tossing the correspondence in the wastebasket, only to lift the card back out and place it on his desk. There, he'd glance at it whenever he passed by, recalling that he nearly took my life, only to save it two days later. He probably thought it odd that I remembered the day he was born. But how could I forget?

At thirty, I needed a tonsillectomy. Years of strep throat and failed antibiotics necessitated their removal. I read the risks and possible complications listed on the surgical consent form. But like most patients, I signed without much thought to the medical warnings and envisioned nothing more than a soothing Popsicle in the recovery room, followed by moderate pain for a couple of weeks. I could not have been more wrong.

After the surgery, I went home feeling as though I'd swallowed shards of glass. My five-month-old son Holden needed my attention, so I rested in between caring for him. The next day, a warm, thick liquid trickled down my throat, followed by the distinctive taste of copper. I called the surgeon's office as instructed for post-operative bleeding.

"Gargle with ice chips," he said.

"Excuse me?" I asked, believing that I'd misheard him.

The doctor explained that a blood clot might be

holding a vessel open and, if knocked off, the bleeding would subside. I gargled the ice, and it worked... for a while. The next bout of bleeding — heavier and faster — increased my worry, and I called the office. I gargled with ice chips once again as instructed, and the bleeding stopped. Later in the day, I headed to the hospital without calling the doctor because the bleeding had increased. Shortly after my arrival in the ER, the bleeding eased.

"It looks like the problem has corrected itself," the doctor said as he looked around in my throat. "I'd hate to stir things up. I think we'll let it be and send you home."

The thought of leaving the safety of the hospital frightened me, but I didn't object. The doctor appeared to be a bit rushed. I noted his dress clothes. "Going somewhere fancy?" I asked.

"Oh, it's my birthday today. We were out to dinner. In fact, my wife's still at the restaurant waiting."

I had interrupted his birthday dinner. Probably made him leave before the arrival of his cake adorned with candles. I suddenly felt stupid for rushing to the hospital without calling for his advice. He instructed me to go home and rest and to call the office if a problem arose.

The next day, I actually felt better throughout the day. I went to bed with a sense of relief, but I soon found myself in a dreamlike state. Swallowing. Dreaming. Swallowing. Dreaming. Gulping. I shot up in bed to find my pillow soaked with blood. I shook my husband awake. The next fifteen minutes consisted of a speeding car, the running of stoplights, and my husband's pleas for me to stay upright. Soon, back in the ER, a hose dangling from my mouth transported my life sustaining blood to a nearby canister.

A nurse stood at my bedside, holding my hand and brushing the hair back from my face. "We're waiting for anesthesia to arrive. They're on call this time of night. We've paged them, and they should be here soon."

"How long?" I managed, watching my life travel

down the hose.

"Fifteen minutes."

"I don't think I have that long." Her silence confirmed my fear.

The surgeon paced outside the room and glanced at his watch every few seconds, failing to mask his worry. My husband cradled our baby in the corner of the room as the nurse continued to hold my hand amidst the unspoken yet palpable panic. The nurse anesthetist from the Labor and Delivery Unit stood nearby, as a substitute, if the anesthesiologist didn't arrive shortly. The gurney suddenly lurched forward and clipped down the hallway as a strange man in scrubs arrived and placed a mask over my mouth, telling me to breathe deeply.

I awakened to the sounds of distant beeps, hisses, and whispers. Too weak to talk, I could only listen as the surgeon stood at my bedside. This time, he wasn't rushed and looked a tad disheveled.

"We were all praying for you in there," he said. "The surgical team formed a circle around you, holding hands while we prayed. We nearly lost you at one point." I nodded, somehow knowing there'd been a higher intervention.

"I need to tell you something," he said, his voice thinning.

He must've noticed my questioning glance. "During the initial surgery, I nicked your facial artery, and it weakened over time. That's why you've been bleeding on and off."

I knew that he risked repercussions by telling me the truth. Perhaps he told me out of fear that I'd later discover his wrongdoing. Or, perhaps, he did so because it was the right thing to do. Either way, I respected him for admitting his error.

He then explained the harrowing night in the surgical suite: the tricky cauterization of the artery the size of a pencil tip, too short to tie off; the impending need to cut my throat from the outside in order to repair the damage if the cauterization failed—a procedure he had never performed before; the lavage to rid my stomach of the large amount of blood; and the prayers over my body as they painfully watched the clock and waited to see if the cauterization would hold.

"I kept thinking about your baby," he said. "How would I tell your husband that you didn't pull through and that your son had lost his mother?"

With the mention of Holden, the realization struck that I'd been so close to death.

"God listened today, and I'm thankful. I pray that you can forgive me for my mistake." He squeezed my hand before leaving the room.

I drifted off to sleep, low on blood and energy. But I was alive. Over the next six weeks, the risk of bleeding still lurked until I had completely healed, but I knew God would not fail me now.

I forgave the doctor for the near fatal mistake during my tonsillectomy and for rushing me out of the ER the following day to return to his birthday celebration. He had stood before God, asking for His help in saving my life, knowing the burden he'd carry if I didn't survive. Knowing my husband would lose a wife, and that my son would grow up without a mother. If God could see fit to answer the doctor's prayers and grant him mercy, I could grant him his wish of forgiveness.

In the years to follow, my appreciation arrived at his office in the form of a birthday greeting. After all, he had saved my life when given a second chance, and he had asked for God's help that night to ensure my survival. And each day, I'm thankful the medical team believed in the power of prayer.

~Cathi LaMarche

April Showers

Prayer requires more of the
heart than of the tongue.
~Adam Clarke

"Winter storm on the way!" the radio blared. I glanced out the window. Dark clouds were already forming above our small subdivision in rural Illinois. Just then, I heard, "Mom! Mom!" In blew my three bundled-up boys and a crisp October wind.

"Mom!" cried five-year-old Robin. "There's a cat down in the ground!"

"Oh. You mean someone's cat's been buried?"

"No, Mom! Please! Come see! She needs help!"

Six eager hands pulled me outside to the curb. "Can't you hear it?"

Yes, I could — a very faint meow, floating right up from the storm drain!

Chat, almost four, squinted down into the darkness. "Maybe we could drop her a rope."

Two-and-a-half-year-old Jay started calling, "Here, kitty, kitty, kitty!"

By now a crowd of neighborhood children had gathered around. "This storm sewer drains across the street," one of the older boys explained. "If we go down to the opening and call, maybe she'll come out."

At the culvert opening, the children took turns shouting, "Kitty! Kitty!" Finally, when Jay called, out she came. Muddy, wet, bone-thin, with a woefully deformed tail. But alive.

"Whose cat is she?" I asked.

"No one's," piped up one of the girls. "Her old owners kicked her down there to get rid of her."

"Well, she's ours now," Robin announced. "'Cause

Jay's the one she came out for."

Back at the house, we wiped the pathetic creature off the best we could. Then, looking around for something to feed her, I filled a bowl of milk.

She ignored the bowl completely and sat and washed herself all over. Now we could see that she was a longhair with striking black-and-white markings. Only when she was immaculate did she turn to the milk. Even then, instead of gulping it down, she sipped daintily, stopping to clean her whiskers from time to time.

"Look at that!" my husband Don exclaimed. "A real lady!"

And that's how Ladycat came to be with us.

Just in time, too. For all night long we were hit with wave after wave of pounding rain. By morning it had changed to snow.

But inside, our home glowed with the joy of a new playmate. For hours on end, Ladycat would play balls, blocks, and cars with three enchanted boys. She blossomed under this love. But two things about her sad past remained: her deformed tail (perhaps broken in that kick down the storm drain), and her need to go outside and hunt for at least an hour every night.

From then on, frozen days rolled into frozen weeks of 10, 20, and 30 degrees below zero. Then on Valentine's Day all three boys got chickenpox—Chat so severely, he went into a coma and had to be hospitalized. His brothers begged me not to let Ladycat out that night, in case something happened to her as well.

But the air that evening was spring-like, with just a little drizzle. "Don't worry, she'll be right back," I assured them.

Quickly, though, that drizzle turned into a wild rainstorm. And for the very first time, Ladycat did not come back. All night long, I listened for her. But I only heard the rain. Until it stopped and everything froze.

The next morning, Don's car slid all over the glass-slick road as he headed off on his long commute to work. But I couldn't call him to see if he got there okay. I couldn't even call the hospital fifteen miles away to check on Chat. Or turn on the radio. Or lights. Or heater. For under the weight of that ice, all the power and phone lines had snapped. Our furnace and water heater were inoperable. In fact, nothing worked but our gas stove. Soon it was so cold inside, the boys had to be bundled up in their snowsuits all day long. It was complete misery with those itching pox!

By evening, both boys had bronchitis. But sick as they were, they kept going to the window, looking and calling for their missing pet.

In the middle of the night, Don woke up in excruciating pain and a grossly swollen abdomen. Even though the house was freezing cold (it was 20 below outside and not much warmer inside), his whole body was afire.

"Don!" I gasped. "I think you have appendicitis!"

Normally I would have called the doctor or 911. But with the lines down, I couldn't even call my neighbors next door. Don needed to go to the hospital right away. But Robin and Jay were far too sick to take out into that frigid air. Don would have to go alone.

As quickly as possible, I packed him in ice, covered that with towels, threw a winter coat over his pajamas, and sent him out into the bitter night — praying he'd be able to make it to the hospital without passing out. Or ending up in a wreck.

By the next day, Robin, Jay, and I all had pneumonia. But so did almost everyone else for miles around. Only the most critically ill could be admitted to the local hospital. In fact, Don had to sit in a waiting room all that night — with a ruptured appendix, peritonitis, and double pneumonia — before they could even find a bed for him.

But finally, after a week, the power and phones returned. After two weeks, so did Don. And after three weeks, Chat did, too. But not our missing cat.

February blurred into March, one storm following another. The same with illnesses.

"It's all because Ladycat left," Robin sobbed one day. "Doesn't she love us anymore?"

"God knows where Ladycat is," Chat replied weakly. "I'm going to pray and ask Him to bring her back home to us for Jay's third birthday!"

On April 2nd, just a few days away? What an impossible prayer!

The last day of March was as white, cold, and dreary as ever. But the wind shifted. And on April 1st, the skies opened up.

"Look, children!" I cried. "April showers! It's raining cats and dogs!"

"Cats?" Jay cried. "Is Ladycat here?"

"She will be," Chat assured him. "For your birthday. God will bring her back."

Changing the subject, I asked, "So what do you want for your birthday tomorrow, Jay?"

"Ladycat. Just Ladycat."

That evening the rain finally let up. Then at the dinner table, Robin suddenly asked, "Who's at the front door?"

"Ladycat!" Jay shouted.

All three boys ran to the door, flinging it open. A biting wind roared in — followed by a tiny, mud-covered creature, barely able to move.

Don jumped up. "Quick! Get her some food!"

But as feeble as she was, the cat slowly, painfully cleaned herself all over. Only then would she eat. Ladycat was back.

The next morning we retraced her tiny footsteps in the mud — all the way to the culvert where we had first found her. Ever since the ice storm — that night she had disappeared — the opening had been completely frozen over. She had been down there the entire time, subsisting on mice and snow, until finally freed by the previous day's warm April showers.

Arriving home just in time for Jay's birthday.

Just as three little boys and God knew she would be.

~Bonnie Compton Hanson

Irish Angels in New York

I've seen and met angels wearing the disguise
of ordinary people living ordinary lives.
~Tracy Chapman

A s my husband, Doug, stood on the curb doing his best to hail a cab, I huddled under the hotel awning with my daughter, trying to angle her stroller away from the cold December rain. When I knelt down to check on her, I wasn't surprised to see her watching the busy New York scene with curiosity. I tucked her pink security blanket tighter against her legs and kissed her cheek where bluish veins crept up the side of her tiny face to her temples.

Frustrated and wet, my husband gave up his attempt to flag down a taxi. Walking back toward me, I saw defeat and complete exhaustion in his expression. I knew the feeling. Just after her first birthday our daughter was diagnosed with a rare brain disorder. Since that moment, Doug and I felt like runners in a marathon race where the finish line kept disappearing.

Doug forced a smile when he saw me looking his way. "It's cab-crazy over there," he said. "I thought I was loud but this Kansas boy can't out-yell these New Yorkers."

We stood for a moment in silence watching people pour out of the hotel, some walking briskly under umbrellas while others joined the cattle call at the curb.

"How's she doing?" Doug asked as he pointed to the stroller. It was a question that was fraught with mine fields, but I knew he was only referring to the chill in the air, not the tangle of arteries and blood vessels that slowly robbed our daughter of the typical toddler experience.

"She's happy as can be. You know Katie, always up for an adventure," I replied. And it was true. Though she had every reason to be willful and fed up with doctor visits, blood draws, echocardiograms and CT scans, she rarely fussed, flinched or expressed her displeasure. Each new doctor meant a different set of toys in the waiting room and the promise of M&Ms on the way home.

A clap of thunder caused my tired, anxiety-ridden body to flinch as the rain intensified. We had been in the Big Apple barely twenty-four hours and spent the previous night trying to pretend we were merely tourists trekking from the Midwest for a fun holiday getaway instead of brain surgery. We ate New York-style pizza for dinner and even stopped at a bakery for black and white cookies, an homage to the famous *Seinfeld* episode. Thirty minutes later, Katie paid her own tribute when she proceeded to vomit the black and white cookie all over my chest.

With only two weeks to go until Christmas, twinkling lights and other decorations were festooned across the city. We marveled at lighted snowflakes hanging from street lamps and animated nutcrackers in shop windows just long enough to forget why we were there. But the enormity of it was always with us, ticking in the background like the countdown clock on a bomb.

Even though Katie wore an ever-present smile, we knew she was running out of time. Despite the gnawing in my stomach telling me something was wrong and my continual pleas for doctors to look at her, really LOOK at her, it had taken months before we received a diagnosis. Finally we had a name for the disorder, vein of Galen malformation, but the prognosis was not good. The surgery to treat her condition was so precise that only a handful of specialists in the world were qualified to perform it.

Now, when it was time to check into the hospital where a brilliant doctor was waiting to save our girl, we were huddled under an awning in a strange city in the rain, waiting to catch a break and trying not to break down.

"Pardon me? May we offer you a ride?"

I turned in the direction of the voice and noticed a middle-aged woman in a long white fur coat looking at Katie and then back at me. Midwestern pride kicked in before I could think and I replied, "No thank you. We're just waiting to grab a taxi."

"It's really no trouble. My husband is bringing the car around now," she countered. It was then I noticed her thick Irish brogue, an accent that warmed me like hot soup.

When a black SUV pulled up moments later, she ushered Katie and me into the back seat before we could protest further and instructed her husband, a tall gentleman with broad shoulders and a full head of snow white hair, to help load our suitcases into the hatch.

Doug and I sat very still trying not to get the expensive leather seats wet with our rain-mottled clothes and checking our feet for mud even though we had been standing on concrete.

As the man pulled away from the curb, the woman asked where we were headed. We knew from our brief time in New York that people preferred short, to-the-point answers so we simply said, "Roosevelt Hospital, please," and settled in for the ride.

I don't know how she knew, maybe it was mother's intuition, or maybe she spied the veins or the dark circles under Katie's eyes, but the wife asked, "Are you going for the baby?"

I nodded my head, choking back a tiny sob as the floodgates opened and we poured out our story. We were only a few blocks away from our destination, but it was a cathartic release and the couple listened intently. Their children were grown and had kids of their own, but the previous evening, the entire family gathered in the city for a holiday dinner and Christmas show at Radio City Music Hall.

At the hospital we thanked them a dozen times for the ride. While I was strapping Katie back into her stroller, the woman called Doug over and placed a laminated card in his hand. On one side was a picture of Mother Teresa, on the other, a simple prayer. She quickly scratched her name and e-mail address on a piece of paper and asked us to contact them about Katie's recovery.

The woman hugged me one final time. After the embrace I noticed her face was wet with tears and shrouded in worry. She promised to pray for us. Then they were gone.

We would never forget that single moment of kindness. As the double doors of the hospital opened with a "whoosh," we took a deep breath and looked down at our girl. It was time to find her miracle.

After three more visits to New York and two more brain surgeries, Katie is cured. During the frenzy of that first trip we lost the e-mail address of our kind Irish angels, but we still have the laminated Mother Teresa card. It sits prominently on our refrigerator as a constant reminder of a tiny ray of light delivered on one of our darkest days.

~Dani M. Stone

My Two-Second Miracle

Blessed are those who mourn,
for they shall be comforted.
~Matthew 5:4

"I saw him! I SAW HIM!"

I excitedly told my husband the news as he asked the obvious question, "You saw WHO?"

"I just saw Donnie!" was my reply, as tears rolled down my cheeks.

I had to sit down. My husband Don looked at me with half a smile but mostly wide-eyed disbelief. We both knew very well that our twenty-eight-year-old son Donnie had died in an auto accident in 1999, and it was now 2007!

As I sat down at our dining room table, I tried to recall what had just happened. Dinner was ready, and Donnie's cat Audrey was on the back of our green easy chair. I had placed the casserole dish on the table and turned to call Don to come and eat when I glanced at Audrey out of the corner of my eye. She was about to jump down from her perch on the back of the chair. She usually joined us in the dining room when it was dinnertime, so it was not unusual of her. What was unusual was the misty form of my son, Donnie, hovering over her with one outstretched arm to pet her! It only lasted a couple of seconds, but he was instantly recognizable with a very big smile on his face! As she leaped down, the vision was gone. Gone in seconds, so that I had to sit and think about this. Did it really happen? YES! I knew it had happened!

Don began eating but I could hardly move my arms to begin my meal. "I was not even thinking about him today," I related. My husband said something like, "Hmm."

"Are you doubting me?" I asked.

"Hon, I have no idea what just occurred, but if you think you saw him…." he began. I wiped my tears and softly said, "It happened. I know it happened. I wish it had not been so brief!"

This was my miracle. After our son died, I prayed that God would bless me with a dream or a vision of him, just to know he was fine and in His care. I had experienced a couple of dreams where I felt my son was there. The dreams left me feeling warm and comforted and truly at peace when I awoke.

This was different. I always had the feeling in the first few years after his death that if I did see him I would probably faint. My faith was not that strong and I was deep in the throes of grieving. I wanted to see a vision of him but at the same time I was afraid.

It happened when I was ready to accept it. God allowed me to see my son, perhaps one last time!

I do not believe he is a "ghost" that haunts my home, as some people might surmise. No. He is in a wonderful, peaceful, loving place and his spirit can come and go as God wills. That is what I believe, and I am thankful God allowed me one glimpse of my son in spirit form! He just had to pop in and check on his cat, and showed me by his smile that he is very happy indeed!

It took some time to convince my husband that I'd had a vision of our son, and he still is not sure why it happened for me. He does, however, know that I vehemently believe the miracle occurred.

I thank God daily for the two-second miracle that left me with such peace.

~Beverly F. Walker

Reflections of Hope in the Snowstorm

It only takes a thought and your angels will be there… for although you may not see them, you're always in their care.
~Author Unknown

I was homesick. My husband, Keith, was attending Utah State University in Logan, Utah. We lived eight hundred miles away from my parents and family back home in Northern California. We couldn't afford to go home for Christmas. We would just stay home in Hyrum, and have a simple Christmas with our baby, Ann.

Then a most unexpected gift arrived in a Christmas card: enough money for gas for the eight-hundred-mile drive home. We were so excited. Keith took time off from his part-time job and we packed the car. We had family prayer, asking humbly for safety and good traveling conditions.

We drove all day through Nevada, over the Sierras, to the west coast of California. Everything went well and we finally drove up the familiar driveway, honking the horn to signal our arrival. My family rushed out to greet us, welcoming us with love and Christmas cheer.

We celebrated Christmas in my childhood home, all of us together again for the first time in three years. My family rejoiced when we announced that we were expecting our second child in the spring.

All too soon, the time came for us to return to Utah. My parents gave us some money for gas. With tears and hugs, we started on our way. Hoping to make good time, we drove steadily through the day.

Toward evening, we arrived in Wendover, on

the border between Nevada and Utah. Snow flurries swirled around the car. We stopped just long enough to fuel up the car. With no credit card and very little cash, we did not even consider staying overnight in a motel.

If the road and weather conditions were good, we had about two hours of driving to get to Salt Lake City. We thought if we could just make it to Keith's parents' home in nearby Bountiful that night, we could rest. Then we could go on to Hyrum in the morning, and he would make it to work on time.

We drove into the darkening night. Frantic flurries of snow swirled wildly about the car. Keith was having trouble seeing the road, as the headlights seemed dim. He pulled over, and got out to brush the snow away from them.

Then he climbed back into the driver's seat and told me the bad news. "We have only one headlight." A simple statement, but loaded with dread.

With another heartfelt prayer for safety and protection, we felt we had no choice but to head slowly out onto the nearly deserted freeway. Our car bravely slogged through the snowy darkness. We desperately tried to keep our eyes on the white line in the road, but it was vanishing quickly in the accumulating snow. We seemed to be all alone on that dark stretch of freeway. There was no traffic in either direction, and the visibility was near zero.

We knew that our parents were praying us safely through the night. We prayed too, for traction and safety.

Suddenly, out of nowhere, a semi-truck appeared, gaining quickly upon us. It splattered a spray of snow onto our windshield as it passed. Then it pulled into our lane, directly in front of our car. Our meager headlight reflected off the shiny silver doors on the back of the truck.

The driver could have sped ahead. Instead, he stayed right with us, lighting our way. The steady flurry of relentless snowflakes dashed against our windshield. The wipers could barely keep them brushed away. The white line of the road was no longer visible. We cautiously crept along, following the truck.

In those anxiety-filled moments, I felt our unborn baby kick for the first time! The miracle of new life growing within me filled us with wonder. We felt that there were angels protecting us that night, and there was a curious peace in our hearts.

Hours later, we reached the welcome street-lights and plowed roads of Salt Lake City. To signal our gratitude, Keith blinked our one headlight at the semi-truck driver in front of us. This man had stayed with us for more than 120 miles on that drive between Wendover and Salt Lake City. Our one headlight had reflected off the back of his truck as he had lighted our way in the dark night.

It turned out that this storm deposited eighteen inches of snow in twenty-four hours, closing the Salt Lake City airport for twenty hours. But we had traveled safely through the massive storm. We offered a heartfelt prayer of thanksgiving for this miracle.

As I gratefully closed my eyes at last that night,

the images of the steadily blowing snow drifted before them. More importantly, though, my mind's eye fixed upon the reflection of the unseen angels and the semi-truck driver who had stayed with us, giving us hope through the darkest hours of that snow-filled night.

~Valaree Terribilini Brough

Soda Miracles

A prayer in its simplest definition is
merely a wish turned Godward.
~Phillips Brooks

One beautiful day in Northwest Arkansas, while visiting the sixty-seven-foot-tall Christ of the Ozarks statue in Eureka Springs, my then-thirteen-year-old daughter asked for a Sprite. Looking at her with barely veiled surprise, I reminded her that we were deep in the Ozark forest, on top of Magnetic Mountain, and that mountain forests did not provide sodas for teenagers. Besides, I could really use a restroom, which also were not naturally occurring in forests, so soda was not high on my list of priorities.

This explanation was not convincing to my dear daughter, who promptly provided a solution. "I'm going to pray for one."

"Sweetheart, one can not pray for soda," I explained.

"Yes you can," she continued, defiantly. "The Bible says to pray for EVERYTHING."

"While this is certainly true, I don't believe God had soda in mind when He handed down that little tip," I reasoned.

"Well, I'm going to pray for it anyway," was her unwavering response.

I told her to go ahead and do so if it made her feel better, but not to be too disappointed if it didn't happen. I did ask her to pray for a restroom while she was at it, and we headed toward the car to drive home.

As we neared the parking lot, I noticed a small building situated not far behind the car. As we got closer, I realized that it was a restroom! How had

I not noticed that before? Well, I guess it wasn't really that bizarre. After all, we were in what was probably a popular local attraction. Regardless of the reason, the sight was welcome!

"Well, ask and you shall receive!" I exclaimed. I asked if my daughter needed to use the restroom before going. She didn't. Tucking her safely in the car, my husband and I headed to the newly discovered restrooms, hopeful that they would be unlocked even though it was the off-season.

"Do you think I handled that okay?" I asked my husband, feeling uncertain about the message I was sending by discouraging prayer, even if it was just for soda.

"It might be confusing for her. After all, you tell her to pray for everything, then when she wants to pray for, literally, everything, you make her feel silly for doing it," he admonished.

"I didn't say it was silly!" I defended. "Just that it wasn't what the verse meant! Doesn't it seem kind of, I don't know… blasphemous I guess? Praying for something as trivial as soda?"

"Not really. The Bible does say 'everything.' Who are we to put limits on that?" was his wise reply.

No sooner did he finish his sentence than we reached the tiny structure that housed the restrooms. And right next to the restroom entrance what should we find but a soda machine? We looked at each other in surprise and moved toward the machine to see if it was even on. It was.

"I don't have any change. Do you?" I questioned.

"All I have is fifty cents," he answered.

"It's a dollar. We don't have enough. That's a shame, since that would have been a mini-miracle to her," I said, disappointed.

"Let's put the fifty cents in anyway," he said.

"What would be the point of that?" I asked.

"She prayed for soda in the middle of the wilderness. Two minutes later we found a soda machine, in the middle of the wilderness. It's worth a try," he explained.

"I guess," I said skeptically.

He plopped in the two quarters, and we instantly heard that reassuring click that signifies the acceptance of full payment.

"You've got to be kidding me. There was already fifty cents in there?" I asked.

And then I did something incredibly selfish. I hit the Coke button even though she wanted Sprite. After all, I reasoned to myself, she'll still be getting soda. Just like she asked for.

When they say that God works in mysterious ways, we all nod our head in agreement. But do we really stop to consider what that means? Not only does He work in mysterious ways, He also manages to use one situation for multiple benefits. The cherry on top is that He can use seemingly inconsequential moments and seemingly minor events to create profound changes within us. This was the day I realized these facts in a new and enduring way. Why such a transformation in foundational thought? Because when I hit the button for Coke, after the machine taking fifty percent payment as full payment, a Sprite dropped into the retrieval tray.

We wordlessly stared at it. I was astounded by the lemon-lime packaging before us, but I think my husband was a bit more astounded by the fact that I had hit the Coke button after what had happened up until that point.

He looked at me. "I think you owe her an apology."

I can't describe the feeling of sorrow and shame I felt in that moment, as humility born of self-realization washed over me. In the midst of my daughter's miracle I had tried to put myself first. What a terrible thing for an otherwise caring mother to do. I was sincerely and completely sorry, and ready to offer my deepest apologies to my faithful little girl. I turned toward the car, prepared to deliver her liquid miracle to her before even heading to the restroom that I increasingly needed to use. Two quarters spit out of the machine.

Tears sprang to my eyes, and I turned to my husband, a sense of awe filling me. He looked at me, retrieved the quarters, and, without another

word, put them in the machine. I reached over and hit the very same button I had hit only moments before. A Coke dropped out.

I handed him the Coke and, Sprite in hand, walked to the car, opened the door, kissed my daughter, and handed her the Sprite.

"Pray for everything, and don't ever let anyone convince you otherwise."

~Sandy Novotny

A Precious Mess

*Every happening, great and small, is a
parable whereby God speaks to us, and
the art of life is to get the message.*
~Malcolm Muggeridge

When I saw Oliver, my teenage daughter's energetic thirty-something youth group pastor, bound up the seven steps leading to the stage to deliver the Sunday morning message, I did something I'd never done before. Turning to my husband, who sat beside my son and younger daughter, I tersely said, "I'm going. Don't follow me."

Oblivious to the eight hundred people who filled

the dimly lit sanctuary, I strode down City Church's outer aisle. Oliver's opening words echoed behind me as I flung open the door that led to the oversized lobby, but I wasn't listening. The glass door that led to the outside banged open after I pounded too hard on its metal bar. I didn't care. I was free.

Heading left, I started walking past row after row of cars until I reached the long concrete drive that led to the main road. I had no idea where I was going. Or why I had left.

Maybe it was because a new wave of grief had crashed over me the night before. Or maybe it was because, during greeting time, the unsuspecting woman in front of me turned around and asked, "How are you?" I should have responded with the customary "Fine, how are you?" Instead, I replied honestly. I had to tell the story I didn't want to share one more time — that six months ago bullying had driven my fourteen-year-old, Jenna, to end her life. Normally I found joy and freedom while worshiping God as I remembered Jenna praising Him beside me and pictured her adoring him now in heaven. Today, however, the tears cascaded down my cheeks.

Whatever the reason, I did know one thing. I wanted to be alone.

Minivans were swerving by me on the busy road as I walked on the narrow shoulder. So, I veered left into the first neighborhood I saw — a subdivision I'd never been in before. On either side of the entrance I noticed a black-and-white oval sign that adorned the towering twenty-foot-high wrought-iron gate anchored by thick brick towers. I was entering Holland Place.

As I walked down the sidewalk of Netherland Lane, my hands stuffed into the back pockets of my thrift-store Abercrombie jeans, I passed landscaped lawns and lofty brick homes. But my mind was engaged in a raw and real conversation with my King.

"I don't understand any of this. I've done every healthy thing I can think of to walk through this grief, and nothing seems to be helping. I don't know what else to do. If I can't see or hear you, you've got to at least show me that you're here. I need to know you care."

I wasn't expecting an answer. Half a mile into the Holland Place subdivision, however, I heard a voice.

"Mrs. Saadati?"

As I rounded the cul-de-sac, a woman dressed in a University of South Carolina Gamecocks navy t-shirt and denim shorts emerged from a grand house.

"Yes?" I answered, wondering who she was and how she knew my name. No one I was acquainted with lived in this neighborhood. "I'm Mrs. Saadati."

"We've never met," she said, "but my son is a seventh grader at the middle school your daughter attended last year. Jenna hasn't been forgotten. The teachers, especially her band director and English teacher, and students still talk about her. Jenna's photos and awards are still displayed. She was so talented and beautiful. Her impact is felt all over the school."

The conversation under the crape myrtle at the

end of the driveway was short. I had no words. Shocked, I simply listened.

"I think of you often and I pray for you," she said. "I haven't forgotten."

"Thank you," is all I could manage to mumble. Before continuing on, however, I asked one question.

"How did you know who I was?"

"I was passing my front door when I saw you walk by," she said. "I don't know how I knew who you were. I just did."

Replaying the conversation in my mind, I retraced my steps. After walking for ten minutes, pondering what had just happened, I reached the entrance with the tall iron gate. That's when I spotted it.

Squashed up against the curb beside the storm drain sprawled something fuzzy and flattened. Road kill, I thought. During my half marathon training runs, I switch to the other side of the street to avoid seeing the smashed critters. But that day, for a reason I'll never know, I did something different. I stopped and crouched down to examine it.

What I saw surprised me. Rather than road kill, it was a run-over, rain-soaked teddy bear. It lay on its back, arms flung open as if waiting and wanting to be rescued.

That bear is a mess, I thought, but I'll bet it's precious to someone.

Then, though it wasn't an audible voice, somewhere in my spirit God seemed to whisper, "You're a mess, too, but you're still really precious. To me."

With tears flowing, I picked up the bear, almost afraid to touch it but not wanting to let it go. I didn't have a purse to put it in and didn't want to carry the filthy mat of fur into the service and explain. So, I cut through the parking lot to place it on my car before returning to the sanctuary.

Along the way I looked up twice. Still teary-eyed, I wasn't focused on anything. But my eye caught a decal on a van that read, "Run… like a girl. 13.1." The distance of the half marathon. The second time I raised my head, my eyes saw a different car's magnet. The picture silhouetted four people — a dad, a mom, a boy, and a girl. My family's new normal. Above it were written the words "Blessed Family."

The crowd was filtering out of the sanctuary just as I returned. I found my husband, who looked at me with an expression that said, "You missed all of it."

Little did he know that God had crashed into my world and filled me with hope.

As I shook my head, my lips formed a delicate smile.

"Wait until I tell you," I said. "God showed up. Even when I was AWOL from church."

~Beth Saadati

Meet Our Contributors

Valaree Brough received her Bachelor of Arts degree in Elementary Education, with a dual minor in English and French, from Utah State University in 1971. She has four children and twelve grandchildren. Valaree enjoys writing, reading, playing the piano, teaching, and family history.

Sally Willard Burbank practices medicine in Nashville. Her book, *Patients I Will Never Forget*, is a collection of hilarious and inspiring stories about her most memorable patients in twenty-five years. Visit www.sallywillardburbank.

com or her blog at patientswewillneverforget. wordpress.com. You can e-mail her at salburbank@ comcast.net.

Bonnie Compton Hanson, artist and speaker, is author of thirty-seven books for adults and children, plus hundreds of articles, stories, and poems (including thirty-four for Chicken Soup for the Soul). A former editor, she has taught writing at colleges and writers conferences — plus loves cats! Learn more at www.BonnieComptonHanson.com.

Immaculée Ilibagiza is the author, with Steve Erwin, of several books including the New York Times bestseller *Left to Tell: Discovering God Amidst the Rwandan Holocaust.* A recipient of the Mahatma Gandhi International Award for Peace and Reconciliation, she travels the world speaking about forgiveness. Please visit her website: www.immaculee.com.

Cathi LaMarche is a novelist, essayist, poet, and

educator. Her work appears in over two dozen books. Residing in Missouri with her husband, two children, and three dogs, she is currently working on her second novel.

Sandy Novotny is a dedicated wife and homeschooling mother with a passion for writing. Describing her life as "joyfully rooted in our Creator," she prioritizes her time in pursuit of His truth. She is currently working on a new blog project and eBook series at www.beconvicted.com.

Beth Saadati is an English teacher and has invested her time and heart into the lives of hundreds of teenagers. She is currently teaching writing classes, homeschooling her son and daughter, drafting two books, and sharing a message of hope in the aftermath of her beloved firstborn's suicide. E-mail her at bethsaadati@gmail.com.

Dani Stone is an author from the flatlands of

Kansas. When she's not writing marketing copy for Lee Media Group or romantic comedy stories, she's probably lost in a book. Dani is proud to be founder of VOGMParents.org, an organization created after her daughter battled a rare brain disorder, vein of Galen malformation.

Beverly Walker loves her time with grandchildren when she isn't writing, Facebooking, scrapbooking or being caregiver for her husband who is battling cancer. She and their cat Maya take good care of him

Cynthia Zayn lives in the Atlanta area, and is the author of *Narcissistic Lovers: How to Cope, Recover and Move On.* She has taught in public and private schools throughout the United States and Mexico City, and now works as a freelance editor for community magazines as she pursues a full-time career as an author.

Meet
Amy Newmark

Amy Newmark is the best-selling author, editor-in-chief, and publisher of the *Chicken Soup for the Soul* book series. Since 2008, she has published 140 new books, most of them national bestsellers in the U.S. and Canada, more than doubling the number of Chicken Soup for the Soul titles in print today. She is also the author of *Simply Happy*, a crash course in Chicken Soup for the Soul advice and wisdom that is filled with easy-to-implement, practical tips for having a better life.

Amy is credited with revitalizing the Chicken Soup for the Soul brand, which has been a publishing industry phenomenon since the first book came out in 1993. By compiling inspirational and aspirational true stories curated from ordinary people who have had extraordinary experiences, Amy has kept the twenty-four-year-old Chicken Soup for the Soul brand fresh and relevant.

Amy graduated *magna cum laude* from Harvard University where she majored in Portuguese and minored in French. She then embarked on a three-decade career as a Wall Street analyst, a hedge fund manager, and a corporate executive in the technology field. She is a Chartered Financial Analyst.

Her return to literary pursuits was inevitable, as her honors thesis in college involved traveling throughout Brazil's impoverished northeast region, collecting stories from regular people. She is delighted to have come full circle in her writing career — from collecting stories "from the people" in Brazil as a twenty-year-old to, three decades later, collecting stories "from the people" for Chicken Soup for the Soul.

When Amy and her husband Bill, the CEO of Chicken Soup for the Soul, are not working, they are visiting their four grown children.

Follow Amy on Twitter @amynewmark. Listen to her free daily podcast, The Chicken Soup for the Soul Podcast, at www.chickensoup.podbean.com, or find it on iTunes, the Podcasts app on iPhone, or on your favorite podcast app on other devices.

Changing lives one story at a time®
www.chickensoup.com